THE ULTIMATE SEX TRIVIA QUIZ BOOK

GW00392689

Ralph Storer

Dedicated to those
who come after us

First published 2019

ISBN: 978-1795499477

Text, design and typesetting by Ralph Storer

Some of the information herein may be subject to minor argument (statistics, for instance, may vary from study to study).

Also by the author:
Baffies' Great Outdoors Inappropriate Advice Column

CONTENTS

Foreplay

FOREPLAY

This is a quiz book for people who like sex.

That means you.

Sex is a topic of universal interest. Everybody knows something about it. Some think they know more than others. Some would like to think they know more than others. Most would like to know more. Here's your chance to find out more and have fun at the same time. But be warned: you are about to have your eyes opened and your mind expanded.

Some of the questions herein are easy and satisfying, some are harder and more informative, some are curious and thought-provoking. Some answers you'll know, some you won't, some you'll think you know but don't, some you'll think you don't know but do.

There are yet others you may not wish to know.

There are those who would prefer to have sex remain a mystery and, if there is one serious point to this slim volume (size isn't everything), it is to dispel such sex-negative attitudes. We have evolved beyond sex for procreation to enjoy sex for pleasure.

So let this book be a celebration of sex in all its diversity. Let it encourage tolerance of the sexual behaviour of others, and let it reassure you that there is no sexual desire you can have that has not been had before at some time and in some place. There is nothing immoral about any pleasure to be obtained from any consensual sexual act of any kind. To suggest otherwise is a travesty against nature.

Finally, may you get as much pleasure from this book as from the real thing (but if you do, there's something you're not doing right).

THE QUIZZES

Trifles make perfection,

And perfection is no trifle.

Michelangelo

1 WORLDLY SEX

1. According to World Health Organisation figures, approximately how many acts of sexual intercourse take place around the world each day?

   (a) One million
   (b) Ten million
   (c) One hundred million

2. Which European state has the world's lowest birth rate?

3. Many primitive New Guinea tribes have traditionally ingested semen. How did they take it?

   (a) Stirred in tea
   (b) Baked in sago
   (c) As a dip for bamboo shoots

4. The ancient Shinto ritual of *kagura* has been transformed in modern Japanese sex shows into the *tokudashi*, known colloquially in English as "The Open". What does either involve?

5. Which country is the nearest country to Britain in which you can join the mile-high club without leaving the ground?
(1 mile = 5,280ft/1,610m)

(a) Holland
(b) Belgium
(c) France

6. Patagonian Indian men have traditionally used a *guesquel* to give their women intense orgasms. What is a guesquel?

(a) A tightly-bound tuft of feathery pampas grass
(b) A penis ring made from coarse mule hair
(c) The penile bone of a walrus

7. What is the Venus Temple in Amsterdam?

8. Which country banned the import of Barbie dolls because they are "a danger to sexual development"?

(a) China
(b) Kuwait
(c) Venezuela

9. Where and when was the first sex shop opened?

   (a) England in 1665
   (b) Holland in 1873
   (c) Germany in 1962

10. What and where is the Nobel Sperm Bank?

Don't call the world dirty because you have forgotten to clean your glasses.

Proverb

2   MEN'S BITS

1. At approximately what age does the penis reach adult proportions?

    (a)   13
    (b)   17
    (c)   21

2. Is the penis more sensitive to touch before, during or after an erection?

3. What is the average speed at which semen ejaculates from the penis?

    (a)   3 miles per hour
    (b)   14 miles per hour
    (c)   28 miles per hour

4. What percentage of men "dress" to the left?

    (a)   50%
    (b)   75%
    (c)   95%

5. What is the function of the prostate?

6. Approximately how many spermatozoa are contained in a single ejaculation?

   (a) 200 to 400
   (b) 200,000 to 400,000
   (c) 200,000,000 to 400,000,000

7. Why does one testicle usually hang slightly lower than the other?

8. On an average night, how many erections does an average man have while asleep?

   (a) None
   (b) 4 to 5
   (c) 10 to 12

9. What is the function of the dartos and cremaster muscles?

10. How many calories does the average ejaculate contain?

   (a) 30 calories
   (b) 80 calories
   (c) 130 calories

3 WOMEN'S BITS

1. What is the average length of an unstimulated vagina?

    (a) About 5-8 cm (2-3 inches)
    (b) About 8-10 cm (3-4 inches)
    (c) About 10-13 cm (4-5 inches)

2. More than 60% of women surveyed report having erotic fantasies during sexual intercourse. Arrange the following fantasies according to their frequency of occurrence.

    (a) Satisfying more than one man
    (b) Being overpowered and forced to surrender
    (c) Acting as a prostitute
    (d) Being made love to by an imaginary lover

3. *Amatripsis* is a term used to describe a form of masturbation available only to women. Describe it.

4. Do breasts contain muscles?

5. The human female is unique among primates in having protuberant breasts even when not producing milk. According to the "genetic echo" theory, why is this?

6. What is the average length of a clitoris?

   (a)   0.6cm (0.25 inch)
   (b)   2.5cm (1 inch)
   (c)   10cm (4 inches)

7. According to the outmoded views of Freud, it is possible for a woman to be frigid even if she achieves orgasm. How come (or not!)?

8. Arrange the following phases of the monthly cycle in the order in which most women have the greatest sexual desire (according to a 1974 New York study).

   (a)   Before/at menstruation
   (b)   Around ovulation
   (c)   At/after menstruation
   (d)   After menstruation

13

9. What part of the external female sex organs is the fourchette?

10. In their pioneering 1966 book *Human Sexual Response*, sex researchers Masters and Johnson noted a "tenting effect" during female orgasm. What were they describing?

   (a) Ballooning of the inner vagina
   (b) Swelling of the breasts
   (c) Contraction of spinal muscles, causing arching of the back

A curved line is the loveliest distance between two points.

Mae West

4 SEXUAL MYTHS

1. What was the original purpose of the English custom of dancing around a maypole on May Day?

2. In ancient Greek and Roman times, which non-urogenital bodily function was advocated for contraception as a means of expelling sperm from the vagina?

3. Why did women in many ancient cultures lie in the rain?

   (a) As a signal of sexual receptivity
   (b) As a method of conception
   (c) As a method of contraception

4. The gingerbread man was once a popular love potion. What was it and how was it used?

5. Before it was known that babies grow from a female egg, the ancient Greeks had two rival theories of human procreation. Describe either.

6. According to 12th century historian Eustathius, why did the Amazons, a legendary tribe of South American female warriors, break the arm or leg of captive men? N.B. It was *not* to prevent escape.

7. According to ancient Chinese teaching, which kind of offspring would result from the union of bisexual parents?

   (a)   A bisexual child
   (b)   A hermaphrodite
   (c)   Twins – a boy and a girl

8. Why did the Victorians object to masturbation?

9. According to Aristotle (384–322 BC), Nature had three ways of generating new life. Sexual reproduction and asexual reproduction were two of these. What was the third?

10. Medieval Europeans lived in fear of being molested by an Incubus or a Succubus. Who or what were they?

5 FASHIONABLE SEX

1. Name the whalebone framework worn by women in the late 19th century to expand the skirt and draw attention to the posterior.

2. The word *brassière* was first used in English at the beginning of the 20th century to refer to a female undergarment. What does the word mean in the original French?

3. Who introduced chastity belts to Europe?

   (a)   The Crusaders
   (b)   The Romans
   (c)   The Spanish conquistadors

4. Name the item of apparel that was worn in Tudor times to highlight the bulge of the penis.

5. What was the kangaroo corset, invented by Inès Gaches-Sarraute in France in 1900?

6. What kind of penile adornment is a Prince Albert, named after Queen Victoria's husband?

7. When did Mary Quant invent the mini-skirt?

   (a) 1960
   (b) 1965
   (c) 1970

8. According to tradition, what item of a bride's apparel is a cure for impotence?

9. What is a merkin?

   (a) A female pubic wig
   (b) A penis extension
   (c) An artificial beauty spot

10. What articles of clothing does Frederick's of Hollywood celebrate?

A lady is one who never shows her underwear unintentionally.

Lillian Day

6   TRUE OR FALSE

Which of the following statements are true and which are false?

1. Man has the largest penis of all primates.

2. At the court of Henry VIII it was customary for ladies-in-waiting (royal attendants) to wear no underwear for the pleasure of the king.

3. Men snore more than women because they have more of the male hormone testosterone.

4. The German word for nipple is *Brustwarzen*, meaning "breast wart."

5. New Guinea tribes tried to halt the spread of white man's venereal disease by holding orgies.

6. Empress Catherine II of Russia had her lovers sleep in the company of boars because the scent of boar sweat was believed to increase sexual potency.

7. Rubbing nitro-glycerine onto a penis makes it shrivel up.

8. Inuit women neither menstruate nor ovulate during the Arctic winter.

9. For sexual stimulation, Louis XIV of France kept a rat in a specially designed codpiece. Tame rats were specifically bred for this purpose by the royal ratkeeper or *Gardien des Rats* – a much sought-after position at court.

10. A cold shower dampens sexual ardour.

*When my love swears
    that she is made of truth,
I do believe her,
    though I know she lies.*

William Shakespeare

7 HISTORICAL SEX

1. What does Valentine's Day commemorate?

2. According to figures collected by a Royal Commission, what percentage of Scottish brides were pregnant on their wedding day in the 1860s?

    (a) 10%
    (b) 50%
    (c) 90%

3. When did Turkey outlaw polygamy?

    (a) 1928
    (b) 1956
    (c) Never

4. What in Elizabethan times was known as "The Great Cleft"?

    (a) A popular pubic hairstyle with a middle parting
    (b) The cleavage produced by Elizabethan bodices
    (c) The vulva

5. What was the 19th century equivalent of the mile-high club, i.e. having sex on a plane?

6. In which decade were an ovum and a spermatozoon first observed?

   (a) 1450s
   (b) 1670s
   (c) 1860s

7. One of the first recorded sex aids was made from wood or padded leather and was known to the ancient Greeks as an *olisbos*. What was it?

8. Of the women questioned for the 1953 Kinsey Report, how many born before 1900 wore clothes while having sex?

   (a) One tenth
   (b) One third
   (c) Two thirds

9. The term "libertine" today describes a morally dissolute person, but who were the first libertines?

10. An 1867 article warned women against the dangers of sexual arousal when using a certain machine. Which machine?

   (a)   An adding machine
   (b)   A sewing machine
   (c)   A washing machine

History is merely gossip.

Oscar Wilde

8 APHRODISIACS

1. Which dangerous irritant made from powdered beetles is perhaps the best known of all supposed aphrodisiacs?

2. The supposed aphrodisiac properties of which eastern herb make it the most expensive in the world?

    (a) Dong Quai
    (b) Ginseng
    (c) Mandrake

3. Some American Indian tribes used buffalo dung as an aphrodisiac. How?

4. Name the popular substance once banned in England because of its aphrodisiac properties. It can be taken as a solid or a liquid and contains the chemicals phenylethylamine (a mood-altering chemical also associated with being in love) and theobromine (in Latin literally "the food of the gods"). The Aztec King Montezuma II drank 50 cups a day to help him service his harem.

5. Which shellfish did Casanova eat to improve his virility?

   (a) Oyster
   (b) Quahog
   (c) Whelk

6. Name the glandular substance that is extracted from the abdomens of certain male deer to be used in perfumery. Ounce for ounce, it is the most expensive animal product in the world.

7. Which supposed aphrodisiac has caused one of the world's largest animals to be poached almost to extinction? To conserve remaining animals, the Zimbabwe government now surgically remove the much-prized part that the poachers are after.

   (a) Elephant tusk
   (b) Hippopotamus tail
   (c) Rhinoceros horn

8. Which popular South American fruit was originally called a "love apple" by the Spanish conquistadors who discovered it?

9. Name the expensive edible fungus, native to Europe, which was prized as an aphrodisiac as long as four thousand years ago in Babylon.

10. What do coffee and tobacco have in common as aphrodisiacs?

Candy
Is dandy
But liquor
Is quicker

Ogden Nash

9   ANIMAL SEX

1.   Which mammal has the largest sperm?

   (a)   A mouse
   (b)   A man
   (c)   An elephant

2.   The male kangaroo has a double-headed penis designed to fit the female's twin-horned vagina. What else is peculiar about the male's penis and scrotum?

3.   On what part of the body is the vagina of a female octopus?

4.   How do male deer masturbate?

5.   Of all the apes, only the female gibbon is monogamous. It has been theorised that this is because it is the only ape that has something in common with the human female. What?

6.   How do female threadworms, secure in their host vegetables, attract male threadworms for sex?

7. Name the creature whose male has the largest penis in the animal kingdom (3m/10ft long and 30cm/12in in diameter) and whose female has the longest clitoris tip (8cm/3¼in).

    (a)   The elephant
    (b)   The giant squid
    (c)   The whale

8. Some female apes practise adultery. What do they have to gain from this?

9. Why does a female cat cry out when a tom cat withdraws after sexual intercourse?

10. The male elephant and male bat both possess a *motile* penis. What does this do?

The ability to make love frivolously is the chief characteristic which distinguishes human beings from the beasts.

Heywood Broun

10   MARITAL SEX

1. What is the origin of the custom of carrying the bride over the threshold?

2. According to a 1951 study, how many of 185 societies around the world were monogamous?

    (a)   16%
    (b)   46%
    (c)   76%

3. The word *nubile* today has connotations of sexual attractiveness, but what did it originally mean in terms of marriage?

4. What was it that, on his wedding night, put Victorian art critic John Ruskin off sex for the rest of his life?

5. Denmark was the first country to make same-sex marriage legal. When?

    (a)   1969
    (b)   1989
    (c)   2009

6. The medieval custom of *droit du seigneur*, by which the king or local lord had the right to deflower a bride on her wedding night, was supposed to be for the benefit of the husband. How come?

7. What are the forms of marriage known as polyandry and polygyny?

8. The largest mass wedding ever recorded took place in South Korea in 1988. How many couples were married?

   (a) 1,357
   (b) 6,156
   (c) 9,728

9. What is the origin of the custom of wedding guests kissing the bride?

10. What possessed Brahman Hindus to marry a tree?

Marriage is popular because it combines the maximum of temptation with the maximum of opportunity.

George Bernard Shaw

11   SEXY WORDS

What is the meaning of the following words?

1.   BATHYKOLPIAN

    (a)   Deep-bosomed
    (b)   Deep-buttocked
    (c)   Pertaining to a sexual practice
        involving Greek yoghurt

2.   URTICATION

    (a)   Sexual application of raw onions
    (b)   Sexual application of whipped cream
    (c)   Sexual application of stinging nettles

3.   HODENSACK

    (a)   A night-gown worn by medieval
        monks to discourage lustful thoughts
    (b)   A Celtic goblin who molested women
        at night
    (c)   The German word for scrotum

4. MEABLE

   (a) Victorian slang for a testicle
   (b) Marriageable
   (c) Easily penetrated

5. BROCAGE

   (a) A pimp's wages in Chaucerian times
   (b) A pubic wig in Elizabethan times
   (c) A type of bra in Victorian times

6. TITILLAGNIA

   (a) Sexual arousal from tickling
   (b) An obsession with breasts
   (c) A compulsion to tell dirty jokes

7. BOGOMILES

   (a) The Thracian god of carnal desire
   (b) Naked medieval Balkan Christian
       heretics who advocated free sex
   (c) A painful affliction obtained from
       certain sexual practices

8. IATRONUDIA

   (a) The state of having no pubic hair
   (b) Daydreaming about being naked
   (c) The desire of a woman to expose
       herself to a doctor

9. MIN

   (a) An Egyptian fertility god
   (b) Tudor slang for the female genitals
   (c) The ancient Chinese art of pubic
       hair sculpting

10. TENTIGINOUS

   (a) Well-endowed (of a male)
   (b) Receptive (of a female)
   (c) Lust-provoking

All words are pegs to hang ideas on.

H. W. Beecher

12   FAMOUS LOVERS

1.   In what way did King Solomon make the Queen of Sheba alter her appearance before he would bed her?

2.   Who was Helen of Troy's Greek lover, whose pursuit of her started the Trojan War?

   (a)   Aeneas
   (b)   Paris
   (c)   Romulus

3.   Which queen, of legendary charm and sexual appetite, had affairs with two Roman generals, later dramatised in plays by William Shakespeare and George Bernard Shaw?

4.   According to legend a queen and a knight became lovers – a sin that in Tennyson's *Idylls of the King* (1859–72) brought about the downfall of the kingdom. Name the lovers.

5. When British admiral Lord Horatio Nelson was killed at the Battle of Trafalgar in 1815, his last words were not for his wife but for his mistress. Who was she?

    (a) Lady Carolyn Lamb
    (b) Lady Emma Hamilton
    (c) Lady Jane Grey

6. Name the 12th century lecturer and his student whose doomed love affair and love letters made their story a lasting romantic tragedy. After their secret marriage was discovered, he was castrated and became a monk while she became a nun.

    (a) Abélard and Héloïse
    (b) Pyramus and Thisbe
    (c) Troilus and Cressida

7. Which of Catherine II of Russia's many lovers became her most powerful minister before his death in 1791? A battleship was named after him and, in 1925, a classic film by Sergei Eisenstein was named after the battleship.

8. Name the tragic fictional lovers whose story first appeared in Masuccio Salernitano's *Novellino* in 1476. The hero poisons himself when he mistakenly thinks his lover is dead, then she stabs herself when she finds his body.

9. What did actor Laurence Olivier keep in his underwear as a gift from his lover Vivien Leigh.

   (a)   A carnation
   (b)   A photograph of her naked
   (c)   A tuft of her pubic hair

10. Name the first of many lovers according to Hebrew legend.

Tell me whom you love,
and I will tell you what you are.

Arsène Houssaye

13   SEXUAL TECHNIQUE

1. The most common sexual position in modern Western society involves the man lying on top of the woman, face-to-face. Why is this position known as the "missionary position"?

2   The *Kama Sutra* describes the "butterfly flick" as a highly effective method of arousing a man. What is a butterfly flick?

3. In their groundbreaking 1951 book *Human Sexual Response*, sex researchers Master and Johnson described four phases of sexual response: excitement, plateau, orgasm and resolution. They also noted a "refractory period". What is a refractory period?

4. The Arabic term *kabazzah* describes a woman skilled in the ancient oriental sexual technique known in Sanskrit as *bhaga asana*, in which the man remains passive during sexual intercourse. What does the woman do?

5. Describe the sexual position that the *Kama Sutra* calls "Reciprocal Sight of The Posteriors".

6. The erogenous zones of the body are those parts that are especially sensitive to sexual stimulation. According to ancient Indian Tantric doctrine, there are three classes of erogenous zone or *marma*: primary, secondary and tertiary. Two of the three primary erogenous zones on both men and women are (1) the genital organs and (2) the breasts and nipples. Name the third.

7. Describe the sexual technique known as *karezza* or *coitus sublimatus*, also known to (and forbidden by) the Catholic Church as *amplexus reservatus*.

8. Name the oral practice that, according to Kinsey, arouses 50% of sexual partners. The *Kama Sutra* lists eight different ways of doing it, including The Line of Jewels and The Broken Cloud, but it could be painful if done without care.

9. What are "Kegel exercises" and how can they improve sexual satisfaction?

10. In 1981 *Cosmopolitan* magazine conducted a survey among more than 100,000 women to discover what accompaniment or preliminary to sex they preferred. List the following replies in order of decreasing preference.

    (a) Alcohol
    (b) Music
    (c) Perfume or body odour
    (d) Sex talk

Knowledge is a treasure,
but practice is the key to it.

Thomas Fuller

14 RELIGIOUS SEX

1. According to the Bible, an aged King David
    lay with a Shunammite in order to restore
    his vigour or "get heat". Who or what was
    a Shunammite?

    (a) A virgin girl
    (b) A virgin boy
    (c) A prostitute

2. The doctrine of "original sin", according to
    which we are all born in sin, stemmed from
    Adam and Eve's surrender to temptation
    by Satan in the Garden of Eden and their
    subsequent discovery of sexuality. Was the
    doctrine formulated before, during or after
    the lifetime of Jesus?

3. Pilgrims flock to the Amarantha Cave in
    Kashmir to see the 3m/10ft tall penis of
    the god Shiva. Of what is the phallic
    formation made?

    (a) Ice
    (b) Rock
    (c) Salt

4. Under Catholic law, what must a prospective pope prove he has?

   (a) At least ten years' celibacy
   (b) Healthy sperm
   (c) Intact genitals

5. Why were Shakers, an 18th century USA offshoot of Quakers, not allowed pets?

6. What is the connection between sex and the hot cross bun traditionally eaten at Easter?

   (a) The hot cross bun was originally shaped like a penis
   (b) Eating a bun was supposed to pardon the sin of masturbation
   (c) Yeast was believed to inhibit sexual desire

7. What was the first religion to celebrate sexuality?

   (a) Hinduism (India)
   (b) Shinto (Japan)
   (c) Taoism (China)

8. Which Pope devised the list of Seven Deadly Sins?

   (a) Peter in the 1st century
   (b) Gregory in the 6th century
   (c) Clement in the 12th century

9. What was the only circumstance under which an early Buddhist monk was permitted to ejaculate?

   (a) After purification
   (b) Between the hours of 8am and 9am
   (c) While asleep

10. According to the Bible, Eve tempted Adam with an apple. True or false?

*No man's religion ever
survives his morals.*

Robert South

15   LIKE AND UNLIKE

What do the four items in each of the following sets have in common?

1.   Desert Shields   Mambas

        Nite Glows   Ticklers

            Clue: ends for means

2.   Elvis Presley   Sarah Bernhardt

        King Solomon   Guy de
        Of Israel   Maupassant

            Clue: number theory

3.   Fratrilagnia   Patrilagnia

        Sororilagnia   Thygatria

            Clue: in the family way

4.   The Fixing of   The Pair
       a Nail   of Tongs

       The Splitting of The Swing
       a Bamboo

       Clue: the Kama Sutra

5.   Mahatma   Sir Isaac
       Gandhi   Newton

       St. Swithin   Florence Nightingale

       Clue: good for nothing?

Which of the four items in each of the following
sets is different from the other three and why?

6.   Cymbalism   Homosexuality
       Lesbianism   Sapphism

       Clue: inclination

7.   Cobblers   Marbles
       Niagaras   Orchestras

       Clue: sexual slang

8.   Deer   Elephant
            Mare   Tiger

Clue: types of vagina according to the *Kama Sutra*

9.   Hexus   Nexus
            Plexus   Sexus

Clue: books by Henry Miller

10.   *Cinq à sept*   Fling
           Flunch   Matinee

Clue: time out

*Man has his will, but
woman has her way.*

Oliver Wendell Holmes

16 UNCONVENTIONAL SEX

1. What can an autopederast do?

2. What did certain African tribeswomen do to obtain what was known as a Hottentot apron or *mfuli*?

   (a) Plait grass into their pubic hair
   (b) Stretch their labia minora
   (c) Wear a belt of animal penis amulets

3. Axillism is a form of safe sex that provides a tight fit for the man but little sexual satisfaction for the woman. Where does an axillist put his penis?

4. Name the painful manual practice at which women in Moorish bath houses were so skilled that some men paid for their services to achieve orgasm.

   (a) Removal of pubic hair by pulling it out in clusters
   (b) Scratching with specially manicured nails
   (c) Testicle kneading

5. In the *cirque érotique* of 1930s Paris, naked women cycled round an indoor track. On what did spectators place bets?

6. What is an Arab strap used for?

    (a) To maintain an erection
    (b) To restrain an erection
    (c) To increase lubrication

7. Which sexual practice in Victorian Britain became known across the Channel as *le vice Anglaise* or "the English vice"?

    (a) Flagellation
    (b) Masturbation
    (c) Sodomy

8. The term *sadism* refers to the practice of obtaining sexual pleasure from inflicting pain on others. The term *masochism* refers to the practice of obtaining sexual pleasure from experiencing pain inflicted by others. *Sadism* is named after the Marquis de Sade, but where does *masochism* come from?

9. In French *à cheval* means "on horseback."
   To which sexual practice did the term
   coitus à cheval originally refer?

   (a) Sexual intercourse on a horse
   (b) Sexual intercourse with an animal
   (c) Sexual intercourse in which one
       partner sits or kneels astride the
       other

10. Origami is the ancient Japanese art of
    paper folding, but what is its sexual
    equivalent – *tsutsumi*?

There is no norm in sex.
Norm is the name of a guy
who lives in Brooklyn.

Alex Comfort

17 ROYAL SEX

1. Which royal personage was the only gold medal winner not to be sex tested at the 1976 Montreal Olympic Games?

2. What punishment did Henry VIII mete out to any male staff who made his female staff pregnant?

   (a) They had to go without ale for a month
   (b) They had to wear hair undergarments for the duration of the pregnancy
   (c) They were castrated

3. Champagne is traditionally drunk from wide, shallow glasses or *coupes*. On whose breasts were these modelled?

   (a) Mme. de Pompadour (1721–64), mistress of Louis XV of France
   (b) Marie Antoinette (1755–93), Queen of France and wife of Louis XVI
   (c) Marie Josephine (1763–1814), Empress of France and wife of Napoleon

4. Wigs were in vogue during the reign of King Charles II of England (1630-85). Of what were Charles' favourite wigs made?

5. How many of the first fifteen Roman emperors had male lovers?

   (a)   Four
   (b)   Nine
   (c)   Fourteen

6. During the Victorian age, the Empress Elisabeth of Austria became much admired for her slim figure. What was her waist size?

   (a)   16 inches (40cm)
   (b)   18 inches (45cm)
   (c)   20 inches (50cm)

7. Which royal personage was pilloried by the tabloid press in 1992 for podophilia?

8. How many breasts did Ann Boleyn, Henry VIII's second wife, have?

   (a)   One
   (b)   Three
   (c)   Four

9. Why did Egyptian queens such as Cleopatra engage in incest with their brothers?

10. How did Empress Wu Hu of the Chinese T'ang dynasty expect visiting officials to pay homage to her?

    (a) By kissing her naked breasts
    (b) By performing cunnilingus on her
    (c) By proffering their penis for her to grasp

I think the vulva of Her Most Holy Majesty should be titillated before intercourse.

> Advice given to Maria Theresa (1717–80), Empress of Austria, on how to provide an heir to the throne.

18 CONTRACEPTION

1. How were lemons once used as contraceptives?

2. With which of the following was the discovery of the contraceptive properties of intrauterine devices (IUDs) linked?

   (a) Camels
   (b) Dildoes
   (c) Drug smuggling

3. Condoms were first widely used as contraceptives in the 18th century, but they had another use before then. What was their original purpose?

4. From which one of the following materials were 18th century condoms not made?

   (a) Animal bladder
   (b) Animal gut
   (c) Animal intestine
   (d) Fish skin

5. Of which three words is "Durex", a popular British condom, an acronym?

6. Until Christian missionaries reached the Solomon Islands in the 1930s, the idea of contraception was alien to the local Bellonese. Why?

   (a) Large families were prized
   (b) They did not link conception with sexual intercourse
   (c) Pregnancy enabled women to take multiple sexual partners without fear of further impregnation

7. In ancient Egypt it came from a crocodile and in ancient Rome it came from a mouse. Which animal by-product was inserted into the vagina to prevent conception?

8. In which French town was a contraceptive museum opened in 1994?

   (a) Condom
   (b) La Pille
   (c) Le Cap

9. The rhythm method of contraception, in which sexual intercourse is restricted to the time of the month when a woman is least likely to conceive, is known as "Vatican roulette" because it is the only contraceptive method approved by the Catholic Church. When was this approval given?

   (a)   1290
   (b)   1660
   (c)   1930

10. What is the most effective method of contraception?

   Contraceptives should be used on every conceivable occasion.

                              Spike Milligan

19 ON THE GAME

1. Who was Joseph Hooker, who is said to have given his name to the colloquial term for a prostitute?

   (a) An American civil war army general
   (b) A wealthy 19th century pimp
   (c) A Victorian anti-vice campaigner

2. What did prostitutes of ancient Phoenicia and Egypt do to their faces to advertise their skills at oral sex?

3. The English word "fornication" derives from the Latin word *fornix*. What is the connection?

   (a) *Fornix* means "arch". Roman prostitutes used to ply their trade beneath the arches of the Coliseum.
   (b) *Fornix* means "facing north". The Roman "red light" district was on the north side of the Tiber.
   (c) *Fornix* means "furnace". Vulcan, the Roman god of fire, was also the god of prostitutes.

4. The Romans defined prostitution as having three characteristics: (1) it was done for money, (2) it was done for the public, and (3) it was done... how?

    (a) By women
    (b) For men
    (c) Without pleasure

5. Martha Jane Cannary was a 19th century American frontierswoman whose occupations included that of prostitute. Why was she known as "Calamity Jane"?

    (a) She shot clients who didn't pay
    (b) She spread venereal disease
    (c) Demand for her services put other prostitutes out of business

6. Ancient cultures practised sacred prostitution, in which temple priestesses acted as sexual intermediaries between worshipper and deity. Where was the oldest recorded temple brothel?

    (a) Alexandria
    (b) Babylon
    (c) Sodom and Gomorrah

7. Why was French Impressionist painter Toulouse-Lautrec called Teapot by the women in the brothel where he lived?

8. Name the heroine of John Cleland's famous erotic novel of 1748: *Memoirs of a Woman of Pleasure*.

9. The French word *essayer* means "to try". What was an *essayeur* in a Parisian brothel?

    (a) A trainee prostitute
    (b) An experienced prostitute who tried out new clients
    (c) A man employed to fondle the prostitutes and so create a conducive atmosphere for clients

10. Name the only American state in which prostitution is legal.

No nation was ever ruined by trade.

Benjamin Franklin

20 SEXY ANAGRAMS

Can you find the words or phrases hidden in the following anagrams? The answer is one word unless stated.

1. USE EXTRA HOLE

    Clue: most people's inclination

2. SURREAL EXECUTIONS

    Clue: what most people indulge in (2 words)

3. I'M AS A MONSTROUS GLUE

    Clue: what many people hope to achieve (2 words)

4. BUST ANIMATOR

    Clue: manipulatory sex

5. ATONAL JUICE

    Clue: a possible end result of 2 or 4

6.   LARGE MOIST PLUMS

        Clue: what some women have
        that most men don't (2 words)

7.   MORE SMOOCHY

        Clue: for men only (2 words)

8.   MY! OH MAN! PANIC!

        Clue: she wants it

9.   SPORT TUITION

        Clue: somebody always pays for it

10.   TRIPLE VOLCANIC PET

        Clue: makes sex inconceivable
        (2 words)

*Many a treasure besides Ali Baba's
is unlocked with a verbal key.*

                            Henry Van Dyke

21 POT POURRI (1)

1. Nymphomania is an insatiable desire in women for sexual gratification. What is the male equivalent of nymphomania?

2. To which James Bond girl's name did American censors object, until the actress playing the part made it respectable by being photographed with Prince Phillip at the film's London première?

   (a) Honey Rider
   (b) Plenty O'Toole
   (c) Pussy Galore

3. *Taint* is an American slang term for the perineum, the area between the scrotum/vagina and the anus. What is the origin of the term?

4. A bigynist and a bivirist both indulge in group sex. What's the difference between them ?

5. What happens to the nose during sexual intercourse?

6. How did the custom of kissing under the mistletoe at Christmas originate?

7. Which food was invented to discourage masturbation?

   (a) Baked Beans
   (b) Corn Flakes
   (c) Muesli

8. One of the two most popular shapes for female pubic hair sculpting is a triangle. What is the other?

9. Why and how were pianos censored in Victorian Britain?

10. At whom did Peeping Tom peep?

Sex is one of the nine reasons for reincarnation. The other eight are unimportant.

Henry Miller

22 POT POURRI (2)

1. Medically, which organs determine whether a person is male or female?

2. In which year did *Playboy* magazine first appear?

   (a) 1943
   (b) 1953
   (c) 1963

3. During his ground-breaking 1940s research on the physiology of female sexuality, what did Kinsey use to stimulate the sexual organs?

   (a) An artist's brush
   (b) A cotton bud (UK) or Q tip (US)
   (c) A gloved finger

4. Which famous librettist/composer partnership wrote the comic opera *The Sod's Opera*, whose characters include Count Tostoff, the Brothers Bollox (a pair of hangers-on) and Scrotum (a wrinkled old retainer)?

5. Which respectable 19th century writer inadvertently wrote in a still-popular novel about a place where "young ladies for enormous pay might be screwed out of health and into vanity"?

    (a) Charlotte Brontë
    (b) Charles Dickens
    (c) Jane Austen

6. In 1940, at the request of Miss Georgia Sothern, American humorist H. L. Mencken coined the term "ecdysiast", based on the scientific term *ecdysis* (moulting), to give respectability to Miss Sothern's artistic profession. What was her profession?

7. J. L. Milton's Victorian best-seller *Spermatorrhea* warned of the dangers of sperm loss through masturbation. Which of the following nocturnal anti-masturbation devices did it not recommend?

    (a) An erection restraint similar to a bicycle clip
    (b) An erection-triggered alarm bell
    (c) A spiked penis cage

8. Pheromones are sexual attractants secreted by the human body. They have no smell, so how are they detected?

9. What was the original meaning of the term "virgin"?

10. Place the following activities in the order in which they are most likely to give you a heart attack.

   (a)   Heavy exertion such as jogging
   (b)   Sexual intercourse
   (c)   Waking up

.

Facts are apt to alarm us more than the most dangerous principles.

Junius

23   POT POURRI (3)

1.   Both men and women are often attracted to the largest muscles in the human body. Name them.

2.   In the spring festival of the ancient fertility god Baal, what was the only way a woman could avoid having to offer herself sexually to male worshippers?

   (a)   By performing a sacred fertility dance naked
   (b)   By performing oral sex on a symbolic phallus of Baal
   (c)   By shaving her head

3.   Which one of the following rules was <u>not</u> in the Hays Code, to which Hollywood movies had to adhere in the 1930s?

   (a)   Kisses must be restricted to 3 secs
   (b)   Couples must sleep in separate beds
   (c)   Women must wear a bra beneath a nightgown
   (d)   While embracing, both partners must keep at least one foot on the floor

4. According to Freud, what is the male equivalent of "penis envy" in girls?

5. Which sexual behaviour was described by sex researcher Alfred Kinsey in 1953 as "physical contacts between males and females which do not involve a union of the genitalia... (but) which involve a deliberate attempt to effect erotic arousal"?

   (a) Kissing
   (b) Petting
   (c) Playing footsie

6. According to English folk lore, what should a young lady do with apple pips to determine which of several suitors truly loves her?

   (a) Bite them
   (b) Plant them
   (c) Throw them on the fire

7. What is the only part of the human skin, apart from the eyelid, that has little or no subcutaneous fat? N.B. The answer is sex-specific.

8. What is the only part of the human body that was designed purely for sexual pleasure? N.B. The answer is sex-specific.

9. What do trichophiles love when it comes to appearance?

10. In which European country is it legal to marry a dead person?

    (a)   France
    (b)   Sweden
    (c)   Switzerland

All debility of man must be attributed to faulty exercise of the sexual act.

From the Taoist text
The Plain Girl's Su-nu Ching

24 POT POURRI (4)

1. How long is the erect phallus of the Giant of Cerne Abbas – an ancient 60m-tall earth sculpture cut into an English hillside?

   (a) 6m
   (b) 9m
   (c) 12m

2. Name the 18th century Italian adventurer, famous for his sexual exploits, whose name translated into English means John Newhouse.

3. Who or what were Titus Perlens, Orchis Extract and Goat Gland?

   (a) Aids to male potency
   (b) Characters in Oscar Wilde's sexual satire *Lady Windermere's Fanny*
   (c) Ingredients used by witches to promote fertility

4. How is the penis formed during the female-to-male gender reassignment ("sex change") operation?

5. How is the vagina formed in the male-to-female gender reassignment ("sex change") operation?

6. In 1967 a North Carolina cinema manager was arrested for showing the supposedly obscene film *Hawaii*, starring Julie Andrews and Richard Harris. Why was the film considered obscene?

   (a) It depicted topless native girls
   (b) Richard wore very tight trunks
   (c) Julie referred to a pair of tits (birds)

7. In modern usage the word *glamorous* describes a voluptuous and beautiful woman, but what was the original meaning of a *glamour*?

8. What are Ben-wa balls?

   (a) Metal balls inserted into the vagina for sexual stimulation
   (b) A slang term for religious orgies held annually in the Ben-wa district of Thailand
   (c) A painful affliction of the testicles

9. One of Shakespeare's favourite puns was "the prick of noon"? To what was he referring?

10. A 1973 study ungallantly divided women into two groups –sexually attractive or sexually unattractive – and then asked them which *risqué* seaside postcards they preferred. Which group preferred postcards that showed attractive women being desired by men, and which group preferred postcards that showed passive men being dominated by women?

*It is one of the superstitions
of the human mind to imagine
that virginity could be a virtue.*

Voltaire

25 POT POURRI (5)

1. What are Hot Rod, Joystick, Swashbuckler and Torpedo types of?

2. Who is the patron saint of virgins?

    (a)   Saint Nicholas
    (b)   Saint Valentine
    (c)   Saint Virginius

3. Napoleon only attacked superior forces if he woke with an erection, believing it would make him victorious whatever the odds. True or false?

4. What is the origin of the term "scarlet woman", once used to describe a promiscuous woman?

    (a)   The colour scarlet was traditionally associated with brothels
    (b)   The term comes from the Old French *escarlate*, meaning promiscuous
    (c)   "Scarlet-coloured beast" was a term used to describe Satan in the Bible

5. The word "pornography" is Greek in origin. What did it originally mean?

    (a)   Sexually explicit material
    (b)   Material written by prostitutes
    (c)   Material banned by the Senate

6. The term "tribadism" is used as a synonym for Lesbianism, but it is more correctly used to describe a sex act that is available only to Lesbians. Describe it.

7. What was the name of the first nudist restaurant in Paris, opened in 2017?

    (a)   La Flambeé Nue
    (b)   Le Déjeuner sur l'herbe
    (c)   O'naturel

8. In how many of the fifty states of the USA is adultery illegal?

    (a)   Two
    (b)   Twenty
    (c)   Forty

9. How many calories does each partner burn during an average sex act?

    (a) 50 calories
    (b) 100 calories
    (c) 200 calories

10. Would you recommend this book?

Do not suppress your feelings,
choose whatever you Will,
and do whatever you desire...
Perfection can be attained by
satisfying all one's desires.

Guhyasamaja Tantra

THE
ANSWERS

Though a man be wise,

It is no shame for him

to live and learn.

Sophocles

1 WORLDLY SEX

1. (c) One hundred million.
2. Vatican City – a state that has been independent of Italy since 1929.
3. (b) Baked in sago. Semen was also used as toothpaste, stirred into coconut milk, rubbed on wounds and used as an all-purpose pick-me-up.
4. The *kagura* is a sacred striptease in which a dancing priestess exposes her genitals to the assembled crowd. In the *tokudashi* a woman encourages the audience to study her vulva with the aid of magnifying glasses and torches. Both rituals celebrate the power of the female genitals.
5. (c) France. The nearest mile-high mountain to Britain is Crête de Neige (5,653ft/1,723m) in the Jura mountains.
6. (b) A penis ring made from coarse mule hair. It fits on the end of the penis with the hairs pointing downwards.
7. The Venus Temple is a sex museum that contains a variety of sexual artefacts, such as a Marylin Monroe mannequin whose skirt blows up at the touch of a button
8. (b) Kuwait. The country's Islamic Law Committee also forbids kissing in public, among other subversive practices.
9. (c) Germany in 1962. The shop was opened by Beate Uhse-Rotermund in the town of Flensburg.
10. The Nobel Sperm Bank is a repository for the sperm of Nobel Prize winners, for use in artificial insemination. It was founded in 1980 in Escondido, California.

2 MEN'S BITS

1. (b) 17.
2. The penis is more sensitive to touch *after* an erection. This can be shown by touching the surface with the two points of a hairpin and measuring how far apart they need to be before they can be felt as two points rather than one. Before erection they need to be 5–9mm apart. During erection they need to be 9–15mm apart. After erection they need to be only 3–4mm apart (the same as on the tip of the clitoris). This is exceeded in sensitivity only by the tip of the tongue.
3. (c) 28 miles per hour (except where speed restrictions apply).
4. (b) 75%. 17% dress to the right and the rest don't seem to mind.
5. The prostate is an organ that secretes a jet of white alkaline fluid in which sperm is propelled out of the penis. This fluid accounts for about half the volume of semen and protects sperm from the acidic environments of the urethra and vagina.
6. (c) 200,000,000 to 400,000,000.
   No wonder men find sex tiring.
7. Nature has arranged for one testicle to hang lower than the other so that they don't get crushed against each other. In right-handed men the left-hand testicle usually hangs lower (and may be slightly larger), and vice versa in left-handed men.
8. (b) 4 to 5. Nocturnal erections occur during REM (rapid eye movement) sleep and are not necessarily related to sexual dreams.

9.   The dartos and cremaster muscles relax and contract to raise and lower the testicles in the scrotal sac, thereby ensuring that they are always kept at the correct temperature (slightly cooler than the rest of the body).

10. (a) 30 calories, making oral sex an attractive meal-time alternative for weight watchers as part of a calorie-controlled diet.

3 WOMEN'S BITS

1.   (b) About 8-10 cm (3-4 inches), but it stretches to accommodate a penis or a baby.

2.   (d) Being made love to by an imaginary lover 56%)
     (b) Being overpowered and forced to surrender (49%)
     (a) Satisfying more than one man (43%)
     (c) Acting as a prostitute (25%)
     The figures represent the percentage of women reporting these fantasies. Apart from (d), the only other fantasy reported by more than 50% of women was reliving a previous sexual experience.

3.   Masturbation by rubbing the labia together.

4.   Yes. Breasts consist mainly of fat cells and glandular tissue, but there are small muscles that control nipple erection.

5.   Among animals the buttocks are the main object of display and attraction. The genital echo theory suggests that the human female breast has evolved to mimic the buttocks in face-to-face interaction.

6.   (c) 10cm (4 inches). The clitoris has a tip, a body and two legs. The sensitive, pea-like tip, about 0.6cm (0.25 inch) long, is the only part that is visible, at the front junction of the labia minora. The body,

about 1.8cm (0.75 inch) long, is concealed by the clitoral hood. The internal legs continue for another 7.5cm (3 inches) down each inner thigh.

7. Freud considered a woman frigid if she did not achieve a *vaginal* orgasm, through stimulation of the vagina, rather than a *clitoral* orgasm, through stimulation of the clitoris. Sex researchers Masters and Johnson overturned this view by stating that all orgasms involve clitoral stimulation. Current views tend towards an orgasmic continuum rather than two distinct types.

8. (a) Before/at menstruation 74%
   (b) Around ovulation (14%)
   (d) After menstruation (7%)
   (c) At/after menstruation (5%)
   The figures represent the percentage of women expressing to be keenest on sex at that time.

9. The fourchette is the point where the labia minora join together at the back, just in front of the perineum. *Fourchette* is the French word for "fork".

10. (a) Ballooning of the inner vagina. During orgasm the uterus lifts up and causes the inner vagina to expand, while the entrance to the vagina becomes tighter and grips the penis.

4 SEXUAL MYTHS

1. Its original purpose was to ensure good crops. Fertilisation of the earth was symbolised by the male element of the phallic maypole and the female element of the dance around it. Until Christian times the dance ended with a free-for-all orgy in the fields.

2. Sneezing. The connection between semen and nasal mucus is perpetuated by nasophiles, for whom nose blowing is a simulation of ejaculation.
3. (b) As a method of conception. Rain, which fertilised the soil of "mother" earth, was often viewed as divine semen.
4. The gingerbread man was a cookie delivered by a woman to a man over whom she wished to cast a love spell. It was usually baked by a supposed witch while the naked woman, sometimes with the aid of a male assistant, reached orgasm.
5. The Aristotelian view was that a woman's body played no part in conception but acted merely as a passive carrier for new life created by male semen. The Hippocratic view supported the "two semen" theory, which contended that conception arose from a mixing of male semen with vaginal secretions.
6. According to Eustathius, the Amazons believed that deprivation of one male extremity would be compensated for by increased vigour in the genital extremity, making their captives better lovers.
7. (b) A hermaphrodite.
8. Bolstered by Church views on the sinfulness of any sexual act that was not for the purpose of procreation, it was believed that loss of male and female sexual fluids, especially semen, diminished vital energy to the point of madness and death.
9. Spontaneous generation. This doctrine was supported by the Church to explain why the Garden of Eden was a paradise for Adam and Eve. Only later did horrible things like flies and insects come spontaneously into being. Not until Louis Pasteur discovered micro-organisms in the 19th century did the doctrine of spontaneous generation die out.

10. They were evil spirits that molested people while asleep. The Succubus was a female spirit that attacked men and drained them of their vital energy, causing nocturnal emissions. The Incubus was a male spirit that seduced or raped women while they slept. Supposed witches were burnt for consorting with these spirits.

5 FASHIONABLE SEX

1. A bustle. In the 18th century "bustle" was a euphemism for posterior.
2. In French a *brassière* is a baby's vest (UK) or undershirt (US). The French word for brassière is *soutien-gorge*, which means "throat support".
3. (a) The Crusaders introduced chastity belts from the Middle East in the Middle Ages.
4. The codpiece – a glove-like appendage that often exaggerated the size of the wearer's own appendage. In France it was called a *braguette*, which today means (trouser) fly and may have given us the word "brag". Not to be confused with a *baguette*, which is something you spread butter on.
5. The kangaroo corset was an S-shaped corset that accentuated the bust and bottom of its wearer.
6. A Prince Albert is a metal ring that is inserted lengthways through the top of the penis. Prince Albert is said to have worn one to keep his foreskin retracted for cleanliness. It was also worn by Victorian men to keep the penis tied in place while wearing the fashionably tight trousers of the day. As a sexual stimulant it gives firmer pressure for both partners during intercourse.

7. (b) 1965. It was sold in her King's Road boutique and became a symbol of Swinging London.
8. A garter warm from the bride's leg.
9. (a) A merkin is a female pubic wig used, for example, to cover missing hair or to change hair colour. In the 17th century the word was used as a euphemism for the female genitals.
10. Frederick's of Hollywood is a museum of lingerie worn by film stars.

6 TRUE OR FALSE

1. True. The human penis is much larger than the gorilla's, even though the gorilla's body is three times as bulky. The only purpose of such a large penis would appear to be female pleasure.
2. False.
3. True. According to a study at Sydney University, testosterone makes the throat "floppier". Women and men with low testosterone levels snore less.
4. True.
5. True. New Guinea tribes did try to halt the spread of venereal disease by holding orgies, with disastrous consequences. Ritual orgies were a common method of seeking help from the gods.
6. False.
7. False. Nitro-glycerine forces blood to rush to the penis and causes an instant erection (N.B. Handle with care).
8. True. Men's sperm count also decreases. Research points to absence of light as the cause.
9. False.

10. False. Cold water boosts production of sex hormones in both men and women. Studies of infertility treatment show that cold baths can double a man's sperm count in two to three weeks.

7 HISTORICAL SEX

1. Valentine's Day commemorates the martyrdom of St. Valentine, said to have been stoned to death around 270 for helping Christian couples marry. The day was previously celebrated as *Lupercalia*, the Roman festival of youth – a day for romance and courtship games. It was common practice for the early Church to take over pagan festivals and substitute its own. However, Valentine was such a popular name that the saint's very existence is subject to debate and the Catholic Church stopped veneration of him in 1969.
2. (c) 90%.
3. (a) 1928.
4. (c) The vulva.
5. Having sex on a train.
6. (b) 1670s. Dutch doctor Regnier de Graaf (1641–73) was the first to see an ovum under a microscope. Around the same time, master microscope-maker Anton van Leeuwenhoek (1632–1723) was the first to see and name spermatozoa.
7. A dildo, smothered in olive oil before use.
8. (b) One third.
9. The French term *libertin* originally meant "free-thinker" and was first used to describe 17th and 18th century intellectuals who rejected the strictures of the Church in favour of free inquiry in the pursuit

of knowledge. Its immoral connotations arose because the Church accused *libertins* of debauchery in order to discredit them. Eventually they came to indulge in the licentious behaviour of which they were accused, but whether this was a conscious reply to the Church's stance is unknown. The word *libertin* derives from Liber, the Roman god of wine and sexual ecstasy.

10. (b) A sewing machine. The article, entitled *The Influence of Sewing Machines on Female Health*, expressed concern about the possibility of sexual arousal caused by the motion of the foot treadle.

8 APHRODISIACS

1. Spanish fly or cantharides. The active ingredient cantharidin has many damaging effects, including a urethral inflammation that causes a false erection.
2. (b) Ginseng. Although prized for its health-giving properties, its aphrodisiac reputation derives from its human shape.
3. They reduced it to powder and drank it in water.
4. Chocolate. It was brought to Europe from South America by the conquistadors, but because of its supposed aphrodisiac properties it was banned from use by the Inquisition. Regrettably, if you eat enough chocolate for it to have any amatory effect, you will be too sick to do anything about it.
5. (a) Oyster. He would eat as many as fifty for breakfast. The historical use of the oyster as an aphrodisiac was based on its suggestive appearance and succulence, but it is also a rich natural source of zinc, which is important in both

male and female fertility and of which there are high concentrations in the prostate and semen.

6. Musk. Musk deer are a small variety of deer native to Asia. In some countries musk is used in food for its supposed aphrodisiac qualities. Experiments show that the scent of musk is the smell most easily detected by women.

7. (c) Rhinoceros horn. In Asia it is ingested in powdered form. Apart from its phallic shape, it contains a urethral irritant similar to Spanish fly.

8. The tomato. In 17th century England the tomato's suggestive colour and texture were too much for Oliver Cromwell's Puritans, who spread scare stories that it was poisonous.

9. The truffle. It emits an odour chemically similar to the pheromone that male pigs emit to attract females.

10. They are both anaphrodisiacs or anti-aphrodisiacs, which act to *lower* the sex drive. Caffeine is a nervous stimulant that can cause anxiety, while nicotine is a nervous depressant that can lead to erection/lubrication problems.

9 ANIMAL SEX

1. None. All mammals have the same size sperm. Only the shape differs.

2. The penis hangs *behind* the scrotum.

3. The head. It's the same tube used for breathing.

4. They rub their antlers against a tree or through vegetation. The process takes about ten seconds.

5. Like the human female, the female gibbon is not subject to an oestrus cycle, which restricts sexual receptivity to the period around ovulation. This

enables her to be receptive at all times, which encourages pair-bonding because the male needs no other partner to satisfy his sexual appetite.

6. The female threadworms stick their vaginas out of the skin of the vegetables and the males crawl around the surface in search of them.

7. (c) The whale.

8. The greater the number of sexual liaisons in which the female ape indulges, the greater the number of males willing to protect her young, because the young might belong to them.

9. The female cries out because the male's penis has backward-pointing barbs. It is the vaginal stimulation provided by these barbs that brings about the release of eggs for fertilisation.

10. A motile penis moves in and out of its own accord during mating, requiring no effort on the part of its owner. The human male looks on with envy.

10   MARITAL SEX

1. The custom derives from the practice of bride capture, in which men kidnapped and carried away brides from other tribes. Bride capture was practised in England until the 15th century, in Ireland until the 18th century and in parts of South America until the 20th century.

2. (a) 16%. Of that 16%, less than one third completely disapproved of premarital and extramarital sexual relations.

3. *Nubile* originally meant simply ready or suitable for marriage. The word comes from the Latin *nubere*, meaning "to marry".

4. The sight of his wife's pubic hair.
5. (b) 1989.
6. Virginal blood was supposed to have devilish properties that could make a less powerful man than a king or a lord impotent.
7. They are both forms of polygamy, in which there is more than one wife or husband. In polygyny a man has two or more wives, in polyandry a woman has two or more husbands. When there are two or more husbands *and* wives, the term used is *group marriage*. In Tibet, for example, groups of brothers traditionally married groups of sisters.
8. (b) 6,156. The ceremony was conducted by Rev. Sun Myung Moon, head of the Unification Church.
9. It's a watered-down version of the old practice of bridal prostitution, in which the bride was expected to have sex with wedding guests before her husband. The practice stemmed from the ancient fear of the blood of a deflowered bride (see 6).
10. Among Brahman men, brothers had to marry in age sequence, the eldest first. To free a younger brother to marry, an elder brother could go through a mock wedding in which he married a tree.

11 SEXY WORDS

1. (a) Deep-bosomed.
2. (c) Sexual application of stinging nettles.
3. (b) The German word for scrotum.
4. (c) Easily penetrated.
5. (a) A pimp's wages in Chaucerian times.
6. (a) Sexual arousal from tickling.

7. (b) Naked medieval Balkan Christian heretics who advocated free sex.
8. (c) The desire of a woman to expose herself to a doctor.
9. (a) An Egyptian fertility god.
10. (c) Lust-provoking.

12 FAMOUS LOVERS

1. He made her shave off her pubic hair. In countries where sex began at an early age, bald genitals had erotic connotations.
2. (b) Paris.
3. Queen Cleopatra of Egypt (c.68–30BC). Her two lovers were Julius Caesar and Mark Antony. Shaw wrote *Caesar and Cleopatra* and Shakespeare wrote *Antony and Cleopatra*.
4. Lancelot and Guinevere. The king was Arthur, legendary King of the Knights of the Round Table, of whom Sir Lancelot was one.
5. (b) Lady Emma Hamilton. Although her husband was dead and she was in love with Nelson, she was excluded from his funeral.
6. (a) Abélard and Héloïse. Pierre Abélard (1079–1142) lectured at Notre Dame Cathedral, where he fell in love with Héloïse(1101–1164), the niece of the Canon. In 1817 Josephine Bonaparte had their bodies reburied together in Père Lachaise cemetery in Paris, where their tomb is still visited by lovers.
7. Grigory Aleksandrovich Potemkin (1739–91). Eisenstein's film was called *Battleship Potemkin*.
8. Romeo and Juliet, made famous by Shakespeare's 1596 play.

9.   (a) A carnation. She sent bunches for the purpose.
10. Adam and Eve.

13   SEXUAL TECHNIQUE

1.   The early Church adopted the patriarchal teaching of the Stoics, which allowed sexual intercourse only in the man-on-top position. This teaching was later propagated by Catholic missionaries to the South Pacific, where local women named the position and ridiculed its passivity.

2.   The butterfly flick is a fellatio technique. The woman flicks her tongue lightly along the underside of the penis. Experts do it without having to use hands to steady the object of their attentions.

3.   The refractory period is the period following orgasm during which further sexual response does not occur. It occurs in nearly all men and lasts from a few minutes to a few hours. In women it is much less common and may not occur at all, making multiple orgasm possible.

4.   The woman "milks" the man's penis by abdominal and vaginal muscle contractions. The technique requires extensive training and modern woman may decide she has more constructive ways of spending her time.

5.   The man lies down, legs apart, knees raised. The woman crouches on him between his legs, facing away from him.

6.   The lips and tongue.

7.   *Karezza* ("caress") is a technique in which both partners refrain from orgasm during sexual intercourse. Its aim is to prolong erotic play. The

term was coined by Dr. Alice Bunker Stockham in 1883, but the technique was practised long before by Taoists, who believed that the quantity of a man's semen was limited and had to be preserved. The Catholic Church opposes the technique because it involves sexual intercourse not intended for conception.

8. Biting (not necessarily involving the breaking of the skin). In The Line of Jewels biting is done by all the teeth (as opposed to The Point, where only two teeth are used). The Broken Cloud is a "bite" applied to the breast, in which the skin is raised into the spaces between the teeth.

9. Kegel exercises (or pelvic floor exercises) were developed for women by gynaecologist Dr. Alfred Kegel in the 1940s. They are designed to strengthen the pubococcygeus (or PC) muscles that surround the vagina. Healthy PC muscles that can grip the penis intensify sexual pleasure for both partners. Kegel exercises for men give firmer erections and greater ejaculatory control.

10. (b) Music, (a) Alcohol, (c) Perfume or body odour, (d) Sex talk. Further down the list of preferred sex accompaniments or preliminaries were (in order): drugs, pornography and food.

14 RELIGIOUS SEX

1. (a) A virgin girl. In many cultures it was believed that contact with young girls could revive the ardour of old men.

2. After the lifetime of Jesus. It was St. Paul in the first century who, amid religious controversy about

when sin first entered the world, linked the first sin with Adam and Eve, but it was the neurotic views of St. Augustine (354–430) that set Christianity's future sex-negative agenda. "Between faeces and urine we are born," he wrote. He linked sin to sex and suggested that sin was propagated from parents to children by sexual reproduction. Hence the necessity for Jesus to be born of a virgin.

3. (a) Ice. The cave contains a stalagmite of ice that has a phallic shape.

4. (c) Intact genitals. At one time the pope sat on a special chair that exposed his genitals to a procession of cardinals, who would confirm their approval by chanting "testiculos habet et bene pendentes". The law stemmed from the prevalence of eunuchs in the Church. The hiring of *castrati* for their singing voices was not stopped until 1878.

5. Shakers were not allowed to have pets because of the possibility of seeing them mate, which might arouse sexual feelings. As in some other religions, sexual energy was sublimated into religious ecstasy, achieved in this case by frenzied dancing or shaking.

6. (a) The hot cross bun was originally shaped like a penis. Roman phallic worship died out slowly in the early days of Christianity and, when the Church turned springtime fertility festivals into Easter, worshippers continued to wear phallic amulets and carry bread baked in a phallic shape. The Church compromised by allowing phallic buns to be carried as long as they were marked with a cross. Since that time the shape of the bun has been modified.

7. (c) Taoism (China). Followers of Tao believed that harmony was achieved by the mingling of male and

female essences (Yang and Yin), each needing the other. While a woman's Yin was inexhaustible, a man's Yang was limited but could be strengthened by absorption of Yin during sexual intercourse, which was therefore encouraged as much as possible. Taoists viewed masturbation as a waste and celibacy as a neurosis.

8. (b) Gregory in the 6th century. His list of seven (gluttony, lust, greed, pride, sloth, wrath and envy) was derived from an earlier list of eight. Of the original eight, Despair was combined with Sloth and Vainglory with Pride. Envy was a new addition.

9. (c) While asleep (or unconscious). One prurient tale of what was permissible told of a monk who fell asleep by the wayside with an erection that was made use of by a number of passing women.

10. False. The Bible refers only to "the fruit of the tree which is in the midst of the garden". In Muslim tradition the fruit was the banana or Indian fig, because Adam and Eve covered themselves with fig leaves. The apple tradition may have come from ancient Greece and Rome, where apples had erotic symbolism and were exchanged by lovers. The tale of an errant female bringing about the downfall of mankind may have been intended to promote patriarchal religion over goddess worship.

15   LIKE AND UNLIKE

1. They are all condoms from various countries.
2. They all claimed or are said to have had more than 1,000 lovers.

3. They are all types of incest. Fratrilagnia is incest with a brother, Patrilagnia is incest with a father, Sororilagnia is incest with a sister and Thygatria is a more specific term for father/daughter incest.
4. They are all sexual positions in the *Kama Sutra*.
5. They were all celibates.
6. They are all descriptions of a same-sex preference, but Homosexuality is unlike the other three because it applies to both male and female. Cymbalism, Lesbianism and Sapphism all describe female homosexuality only.
7. They are all slang for testicles, but Marbles is unlike the other three because it is not *rhyming* slang: Cobblers' *Awls*, Niagara *Falls*, Orchestra *Stalls*.
8. They are all types of vagina, except Tiger. The Deer has a capacity of six finger widths, the Mare nine finger widths and the Elephant twelve finger widths. According to the *Kama Sutra*, it is possible to tell the type from a woman's outward appearance.
9. They are all books by Henry Miller, except Hexus.
10. They are all colloquial terms for sexual liaisons, but Fling is unlike the other three because it is not restricted to a short, specific time of the day. A *Cinq à sept* takes place in the early evening, a Matinee takes place in the afternoon and what happens at a Flunch requires little stretch of the imagination.

16 UNCONVENTIONAL SEX

1. He can insert his penis into his own anus.
2. (b) Stretch their labia minora. The women of African tribes such as the Baganda and the Bagishu achieved the *mfuli* by pulling or by tying the labia

together and dangling a rock from them. For everyday tasks the labia, often several inches long, were tucked out of the way into the vagina. The genital modification was highly prized by the men.

3.   An axillist puts his penis in his partner's armpit. A shaven armpit is said to be more arousing than a hairy armpit, but designer stubble can be painful.

4.   (a) Pulling out of pubic hair in clusters.

5.   Spectators bet on which woman could reach orgasm first from saddle gyration.

6.   (a) An Arab strap is a ring that fits around the base of the penis to maintain an erection.

7.   (a) Flagellation. The practice of flagellation for sexual arousal has a long history but became more prevalent in Victorian Britain after caning became a common form of school punishment.

8.   *Masochism* is named after Leopold von Sacher-Masoch. De Sade (1740–1814) and Sacher-Masoch (1835–95) were novelists who wrote respectively about practices involving the inflicting and receiving of pain for sexual pleasure. Their names were later used to describe such practices.

9.   (a) *Coitus à cheval* originally referred literally to sexual intercourse on a horse. The rocking gait of the horse provided impetus and rhythm.

10.   *Tsutsumi* is the ancient Japanese art of packaging the penis to offer as a gift to the lover. Intricate designs concocted with silk and ribbons made unwrapping arousing for both partners.

17 ROYAL SEX

1. Princess Anne, who won a gold medal as a member of the British equestrian team.
2. (a) They had to go without ale for a month.
3. (b) Marie Antoinette (allegedly).
4. The pubic hairs of his mistresses.
5. (c) Fourteen. Only Claudius was heterosexual.
6. (a) 16 inches (40cm). She was aided by the fashionable but inhibitingly tight corsets of the age, from where the expression "strait-laced" comes.
7. Sarah Ferguson, Duchess of Kent. Podophilia is an attraction to or fetish for feet. While estranged from her husband Prince Andrew, she was photographed having her toes sucked by another man.
8. (b) Three. She also had six fingers on each hand.
9. The Egyptians based succession to the throne on matrilineal ties (i.e. to the mother rather than the father), because paternity could never be proved. Therefore the only way a son could rule was by marrying his sister. Ptolemy was married to his sister Cleopatra when he was 10 and she was 14.
10. (b) By performing cunnilingus on her. Paintings depict the empress standing open-robed while her visitors kneel before her and pay their respects.

18 CONTRACEPTION

1. A half-lemon was inserted into the vagina like a diaphragm. As well as being a barrier to sperm, its acidity acted as a spermicide. Casanova was a well-known lemon advocate.

2. (a) Camels. Arab camel drivers discovered that inserting a stone into a female camel's uterus prevented the camel from becoming fertile during long desert crossings. How they discovered this is not known… and perhaps it should stay that way.

3. The original purpose of the condom was to protect the wearer from syphilis. The term "prophylactic", which is sometimes used as a synonym for condom, means "protecting from disease". Casanova was a well-known condom advocate.

4. (a) Animal bladder. Sheep gut was the most common condom material, but the intestines of other animals and materials such as fish skin were also used. The modern condom did not appear until after the invention of vulcanised rubber in the 1840s.

5. "Durex" is an acronym of DUrable, REliable, eXcellent.

6. (b) The Bellonese did not understand the idea of contraception because they did not understand the mechanics of conception. They believed that children were sent by ancestral deities and that sexual intercourse was purely for pleasure. The missionaries soon put an end to that.

7. Dung. It may have been used compacted as a cervical plug, or in more viscous form to soak up or reduce the mobility of sperm. On the other hand, perhaps the process of applying it was enough to deter potential suitors.

8. (a) Condom, in south-west France.

6. (c) 1930. The Catholic Church approved the rhythm method following breakthroughs in 1920s in the understanding of the menstrual cycle.

10. Sexual abstinence – the only 100% effective contraceptive method.

19 ON THE GAME

1. (a) General Joseph "Fightin' Joe" Hooker (1814–79) was an American general. The use of his name as a colloquial term for prostitute may derive from his penchant for prostitutes during the California Gold Rush or from the women that followed his brigade during the civil war.
2. Apply lipstick. This may have been the original purpose of lipstick, although another explanation of its origin is that it was invented to mimic the sexual arousal of the genital labia.
3. (a) *Fornix* means "arch".
4. (c) Without pleasure.
5. (b) Her nickname is said to derive from the venereal diseases she spread among her clients.
6. (b) Babylon, c.2000 BC. Every Babylonian woman entered the temple of Ishtar, the goddess of sexuality, at least once in her life in order to become a temporary sacred prostitute. The occupation held no stigma but incensed the Hebrews of the Old Testament, who named the city of Babylon "the great whore".
7. Owing to a medical condition, he had a hunched back and an oversized penis.
8. Fanny Hill. Cleland was prosecuted for 'corrupting the morals of the king's subjects', but he apologised and the case was dropped. The book was banned in the UK until 1963 and in the USA until 1966.
9. (c) A man employed to fondle the prostitutes.
10. Nevada. Prostitution was not technically illegal anywhere in the USA until it was outlawed in the early 20th century. It was legalised in Nevada in

1973 but only in brothels in 12 out of 17 counties and not in Las Vegas.

20   SEXY ANAGRAMS

1. Heterosexual.
2. Sexual intercourse.
3. Simultaneous orgasm.
4. Ejaculation.
5. Multiple orgasms.
6. Y chromosome.
7. Nymphomaniac.
8. Prostitution.
9. Masturbation.
10. Contraceptive pill.

21   POT POURRI (1)

1. The male equivalent of nymphomania is *satyriasis*, named after the part-human, part-goat satyrs of Greek mythology, who had an insatiable sex drive. A generic term for both nymphomania and satyriasis is *erotomania*.
2. (c) Pussy Galore in *Goldfinger* (1964). Her name was about to be changed to Kitty Galore until producer Cubby Broccoli convinced the American censors that what was good enough for Prince Phillip was good enough for the American public.
3. It ain't one thing or the other.
4. A bigynist is a man who indulges with two women, whereas a bivirist is a woman who indulges with two men.

5.   The nasal tissues swell, causing a blocked or runny nose, known in folklore as "honeymoon nose".

6.   It's a watered-down version of racier goings-on that used to take place during the Roman winter festival of Saturnalia before the Church assimilated it as Christmas. While red holly berries are a symbol of menstrual blood, mistletoe is traditionally associated with magical power and sexual potency. The white berries represent drops of semen.

7.   (b) Corn Flakes. Dr. John Harvey Kellogg was a misguided but zealous believer in the dangers of masturbation, which he held responsible for everything from acne to insanity. Believing that the practice was encouraged by spicy food, he invented Corn Flakes as an anti-masturbation cereal.

8.   A heart.

9.   To prevent piano legs arousing men because of their resemblance to women's legs, they were covered in baggy linen (the piano legs, that is, not the men).

10. According to legend, Peeping Tom peeped at Lady Godiva (c.1040–80), wife of Leofric, Earl of Mercia. Leofric rashly promised to reduce taxes if his wife rode naked through the streets of Coventry. Everyone stayed indoors but Tom took a peek and was struck blind for his effrontery.

22 POT POURRI (2)

1.   The gonads. If the gonads are testicles the person is male, if the gonads are ovaries the person is female, regardless of the appearance of the outward genital organs.

2. (b) 1953. At its peak in the early 1970s it sold seven million copies a month.
3. (b) A cotton bud or Q tip.
4. Gilbert and Sullivan. The opera was never publicly performed.
5. (c) Jane Austen. The 1816 novel was *Emma*.
6. She was a "striptease artist". Mencken equated her removal of feathers with moulting.
7. (a) An erection restraint similar to a bicycle clip.
8. Pheromones enter the nose but bypass the olfactory system and so are not smelt. Instead they are detected by the vomeronasal organ (a pair of tiny pits in the nose's dividing wall) and diffused directly to the brain.
9. A virgin was originally any girl or woman who was not bound to any man. It was in this sense that goddesses such as the Greek Artemis (Roman Diana), goddess of the hunt, were "virgin goddesses". Only when patriarchal marriage became the norm and husbands demanded an "untouched" bride did virginity begin to assume its modern meaning. In many old languages the word for "virgin" and "maiden" was the same, which caused all sorts of misunderstandings about "virgin births" for later religions.
10. (c) Waking up (10%), (a) Heavy exertion such as jogging (4%), (b) Sexual intercourse (1%). The figures refer to the percentage of heart attacks caused by each activity, according to a study by Harvard Medical School.

23 POT POURRI (3)

1. The gluteal muscles, i.e. the buttocks.
2. (c) By shaving her head.
3. (c) Women must wear a bra beneath a nightgown. The Hays Code was not abandoned until the 1960s.
4. Castration complex. Feminist theory suggests that what Freud regarded as envy *of* the penis was more likely to be simple interest *in* the penis.
5. (b) Petting.
6. (c) For each suitor she throws a pip on the fire. If the pip makes no noise then the associated suitor is not truly in love with her, but if the pip pops then he too is bursting with love for her.
7. The skin of the scrotum.
8. The clitoris. Despite prolonged investigation by generations of male scientists, no function for the clitoris has been found other than female pleasure.
9. Hairiness. The opposite of trichophilia, i.e. a love of hairlessness, is acomoclitism. Julius Caesar noted that "the Britons shave every part of their body except their head and upper lip".
10. (a) France. The first posthumous marriage (necrogamy) took place following a 1959 flood disaster. Moved by a grieving woman, President de Gaulle had the ceremony written into the civil code to allow her to marry her late fiancé. Another prominent posthumous marriage took place in 2017 between a man and his male partner – a policeman killed during the terrorist attack on the Bataclan theatre in Paris.

24 POT POURRI (4)

1. (c) 12m. The phallus reaches up to the giant's chest. In olden days women wishing to become pregnant would sleep on it overnight.
2. Giovanni Casanova. *Casa* = house and *nuova* = new in Italian.
3. (a) They were supposed aids to male potency that appeared on the market in the early 20th century.
4. The penis is gutted and the skin is turned inside out to form the lining of a vagina in the vicinity of the perineum. The urethral opening is placed just above the new vaginal opening. The testicles are removed and the scrotal sac becomes the labia.
5. The urethra is extended by means of a catheter, which is then covered with skin from the abdomen to form the penis body.
6. (a) It depicted topless (native) girls, which was illegal according to an old local law that pre-dated the advent of cinema.
7. A glamour was originally a magic spell that witches were said to cast on a man to cause him to imagine that he had lost his penis. The testimony of men afflicted by such hysteria caused women to suffer horrible deaths as supposed witches. In Scotland *glamour* became a synonym for *grammar* because the occult was associated with learning.
8. (a) Ben-wa balls are two metal balls inserted into the vagina to provide sexual stimulation while walking. It is said that hollow centres with mobile weights provide the best results.
9. The midday sundial, whose shadow he equated to an erection.

10. The "attractive" women preferred postcards that showed passive men being dominated by women, while the "unattractive" women preferred postcards that showed attractive women being desired by men.

25 POT POURRI (5)

1. They are all types of vibrator.
2. (a) Saint Nicholas.
3. False.
4. (c) The term comes from a description by St. John of an unholy woman in the Bible's Book of Revelation: "I saw a woman sit upon a scarlet-coloured beast, full of names of blasphemy..."
5. (b) Material written by prostitutes.
6. Tribadism is the rubbing together of pubic mounds for mutual clitoral stimulation.
7. (c) O'naturel. It had to close in 2019 owing to lack of bums on seats.
8. (b) Twenty. Old adultery laws favouring men still lie on many statute books from a time when marriage and inheritance was male-dominated. The laws are gradually being repealed. Massachusetts was the latest state to repeal its law in 2018.
9. (b) During an average sex act each partner burns only 100 calories, but no-one said you have to be average.
10. Yes!

Printed in Great Britain
by Amazon

71756874R00061